CELEBRATING OUR COMMUNITIES

CELEBRATING ALL RELIGIONS

BY ABBY COLICH

BLUE OWL
BOOKS

TIPS FOR CAREGIVERS

Social and emotional learning (SEL) helps children manage emotions, learn how to feel empathy, create and achieve goals, and make good decisions. Strong lessons and support in SEL will help children establish positive habits in communication, cooperation, and decision-making. By incorporating SEL in early reading, children will learn the importance of accepting and celebrating all people in their communities.

BEFORE READING

Talk to the reader about religion. Explain that religion has to do with beliefs. Explain that the world is full of many different religious beliefs.

Discuss: Do you practice a religion? Can you explain what your religion believes? Can you name any other religions?

AFTER READING

Talk to the reader about ways he or she can celebrate or respect different religions.

Discuss: What is one way you can respect another person's religious beliefs? Why is it good for a community to respect all beliefs?

SEL GOAL

Children may have heard to not make fun of or exclude others for being different, but they may not understand why. Talk to readers about the importance of empathy in accepting and celebrating the differences of others. Have they ever felt singled out for having different beliefs? What did it feel like? If they haven't experienced this, ask them to imagine what it feels like. Make a list of these different feelings. Then ask readers to list the feelings they have when they are included and accepted. Explain that our communities are better when everyone is accepted and included.

TABLE OF CONTENTS

CHAPTER 1

WHAT IS RELIGION?

Does your family practice a **religion**? Maybe you practice more than one or none at all.

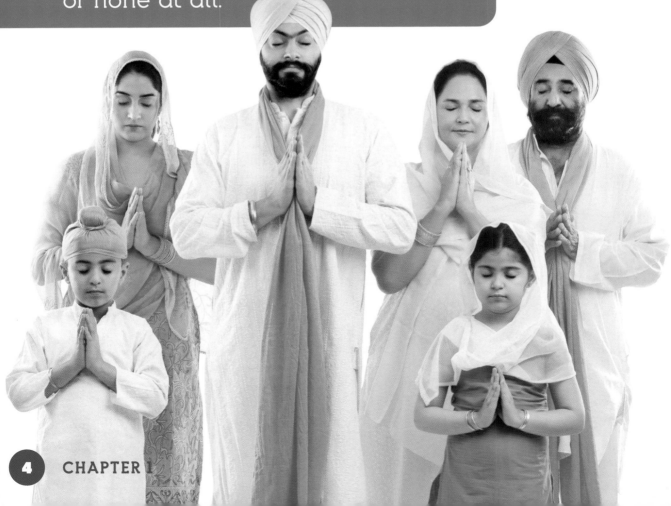

Religion has to do with **beliefs**. Our beliefs are important to us. We don't all have the same beliefs. But we do all have the right to believe what we want.

Your **community** may have many different religions. Learn what the beliefs of those religions are. Are they different from yours? Our communities are stronger when we understand one another.

WE ALL HAVE BELIEFS

What do you believe? Even if you don't follow a religion, you probably have beliefs. Do you think you should always tell the truth? Do you think it's important to be kind? These are beliefs!

CHAPTER 2

HOW WE PRACTICE

Does your family celebrate religious holidays? Kai is Buddhist. He celebrates Vesak. He **honors** Buddha by pouring water on a statue.

Bina is Hindu. She celebrates Holi and the welcoming of spring. She and her friends throw colored powder on each other to celebrate!

The world is full of many different religions. We all celebrate in different ways. Most religions believe in a **god** or gods. People may **worship** these gods. Chloe is Jewish. She believes in one god. Dev is Hindu. He believes in many gods.

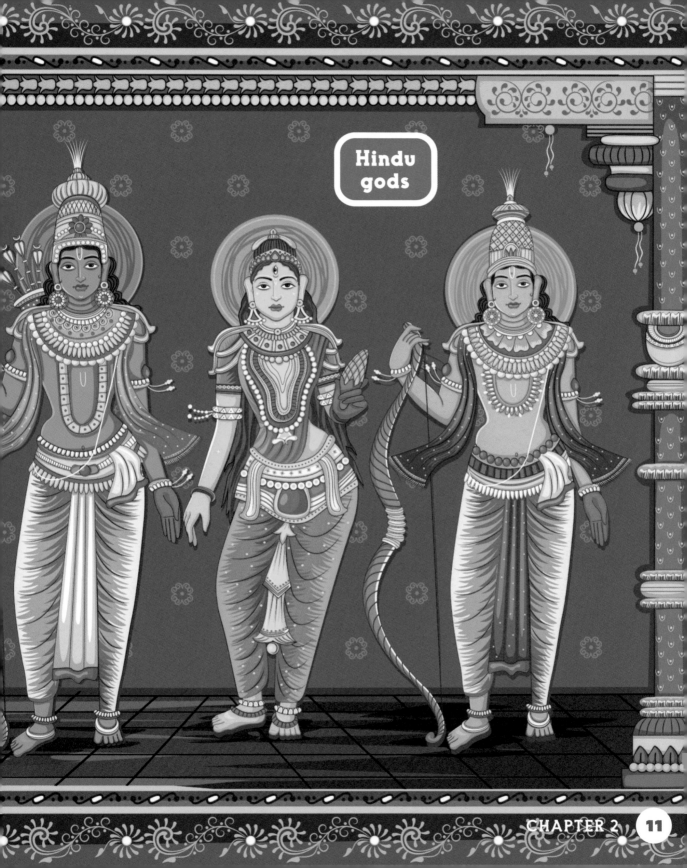

Hindu gods

People may **pray** to a god or gods.
Cora is Christian. She prays to God.
Naji is Muslim. He prays to God, too.
He calls God Allah.

Some religions have weekly **services** or celebrations. Hattie is Jewish. Her family celebrates Shabbat every weekend. Julie is Christian. She goes to **church** with her family every Sunday. Omar is Muslim. He prays in a **mosque** on Fridays. Their religions are different, but they all take time to celebrate. This time is important to them.

PRACTICING FAITH

Religion is a huge part of some people's lives. They may pray and go to services often. For others, religion is only a small part of their lives. They may only practice parts of it every now and then. People show and practice their **faith** in different ways.

Shabbat

CHAPTER 3

RESPECT ALL BELIEFS

Religion is only one part of people's lives. Talk to someone with different religious beliefs. You may find out you have a lot in common. Do you both like to garden?

Maybe you both enjoy playing cards. There is so much more to people than their beliefs. When you find what you have in common with others, it's easier to **accept** and understand them.

Sikh temple

One religion or belief is not better than another. They all deserve respect. Choosing not to follow a religion is also a belief. That deserves respect, too.

One way to show respect for someone's beliefs is to ask him or her about them. Ari doesn't practice a religion. His friend Dillon is Sikh. They talk about their beliefs. Ari visits the Sikh **temple** with Dillon. He learns more about the religion.

KEEP AN OPEN MIND

If you go to a religious service, some things may seem different or unusual to you. Don't judge. Never tease or make fun of people for what they believe. You don't have to follow the same beliefs, but you should respect them.

It is normal to feel confused by something that is **unfamiliar**. But you should respect others, no matter their religion or beliefs. We can gain understanding by being brave enough to ask questions! This helps us accept others.

When you accept and respect others, it helps everyone get along. And that is great for your community!

GOALS AND TOOLS

GROW WITH GOALS

Accepting all people, no matter their religion or beliefs, is important. Understanding people's beliefs and getting to know them outside of their beliefs will help you accept others.

Goal: Learn something new about a religion or someone's beliefs. Are any of their beliefs similar to yours? Which beliefs are different? How do you feel about it?

Goal: What is one way you can be more accepting of others' religious beliefs? How can you try to do this more often?

Goal: Get to know someone new. Try to find one thing you have in common or that you both like.

WRITING REFLECTION

Understanding your own beliefs can help you understand and accept those around you.

1. What are your beliefs?

2. What is one thing about another religion or someone else's beliefs you want to learn more about?

3. What is one thing you can do to be more accepting of others' beliefs?

GLOSSARY

accept
To agree that something is correct, satisfactory, or enough.

beliefs
Things people believe to be true, or the ideas that, together, form a religion.

church
A building used by Christians for worship.

community
A group of people who all have something in common.

faith
Belief in a god or gods or in a system or religion.

god
A superhuman being who is worshipped.

honors
Praises someone or something.

mosque
A building used by Muslims for worship.

pray
To talk to a god to give thanks or ask for help.

religion
A specific system of beliefs, faith, and worship.

services
Ceremonies of religious worship.

temple
A building used for worship.

unfamiliar
Not well known or easily recognized.

worship
To show love and devotion to a god or gods, especially by praying or going to a religious service.

TO LEARN MORE

FACT SURFER

Finding more information is as easy as 1, 2, 3.

1. Go to www.factsurfer.com

2. Enter "**celebratingallreligions**" into the search box.

3. Choose your cover to see a list of websites.

INDEX

Blue Owl Books are published by Jump!, 5357 Penn Avenue South, Minneapolis, MN 55419, www.jumplibrary.com

Copyright © 2021 Jump! International copyright reserved in all countries. No part of this book may be reproduced in any form without written permission from the publisher.

Library of Congress Cataloging-in-Publication Data

Names: Colich, Abby, author.
Title: Celebrating all religions / Abby Colich.
Description: Minneapolis, MN: Jump!, Inc., 2021.
Series: Celebrating our communities | Includes index.
Audience: Ages 7–10 | Audience: Grades 2–3
Identifiers: LCCN 2020002150 (print)
LCCN 2020002151 (ebook)
ISBN 9781645273745 (hardcover)
ISBN 9781645273752 (paperback)
ISBN 9781645273769 (ebook)
Subjects: LCSH: Religion–Juvenile literature. | Religions–Juvenile literature. | Children–Religious life–Juvenile literature.
Classification: LCC BL48 .C5635 2021(print) | LCC BL48 (ebook) | DDC 200–dc23
LC record available at https://lccn.loc.gov/2020002150
LC ebook record available at https://lccn.loc.gov/2020002151

Editor: Jenna Gleisner
Designer: Michelle Sonnek

Photo Credits: MidoSemsem/Shutterstock, cover (right); VaLiza/Shutterstock, cover (left); studerga/iStock, 1; Ebtikar/Shutterstock, 3; Hemant Mehta/SuperStock, 4; Pixel-Shot/Shutterstock, 5; Wavebreakmedia/Shutterstock, 6–7; Chris JUNG/Alamy, 8; Nikada/iStock, 9; PremiumStock/Shutterstock, 10–11; IndiaPicture/Getty, 12–13; Monkey Business Images/Shutterstock, 14–15; Boris Ryaposov/Shutterstock, 16 (left); Kues/Shutterstock, 16 (right); yacobchuk/iStock, 17; AGF Srl/Alamy, 18–19; Wavebreakmedia/iStock, 20–21.

Printed in the United States of America at Corporate Graphics in North Mankato, Minnesota.